The Story
of a
Story

Deborah Hopkinson
Pictures by Hadley Hooper

NEAL PORTER BOOKS
HOLIDAY HOUSE / NEW YORK

For Oliver,
tell stories! —D.H.

For all those who have stuck with it —H.H.

Neal Porter Books

Text copyright © 2021 by Deborah Hopkinson
Illustrations copyright © 2021 by Hadley Hooper
All Rights Reserved
HOLIDAY HOUSE is registered in the U.S. Patent and Trademark Office.
Printed and bound in June 2021 at C&C Offset, Shenzhen, China.
The artwork for this book was created with pen, ink, and paint and finished in Photoshop.
Book design by Jennifer Browne
www.holidayhouse.com
First Edition
1   3   5   7   9   10   8   6   4   2

Library of Congress Cataloging-in-Publication Data

Names: Hopkinson, Deborah, author. | Hooper, Hadley, illustrator.
Title: The story of a story / by Deborah Hopkinson ; illustrated by Hadley
Hooper.
Description: First edition. | New York : Holiday House, [2021] | Audience:
Ages 4 to 8. | Audience: Grades K–1. | Summary: A child struggles to
write a story until he finds inspiration outside his window.
Identifiers: LCCN 2020044122 | ISBN 9780823444915 (hardcover)
Subjects: CYAC: Authorship—Fiction.
Classification: LCC PZ7.H778125 Sv 2021 | DDC [E]—dc23
LC record available at https://lccn.loc.gov/2020044122

ISBN: 978-0-8234-4491-5 (hardcover)

This is the story of a story.

You arrive

with a pencil or two,
a big eraser,
your favorite pencil sharpener,
and a snack
(a healthy one).

And, of course, you bring your eyes and ears,
nose and fingers.

You bring your mind and heart,
your endless curiosity,
and a deep longing

to create, to write,

to say something about the world—to tell a story.

You bring all the invisible things
that make you . . .
you.

For a long time,
     nothing much happens.

Except for some apple chewing,
and two broken pencils.

And after a while there's . . .

. . . a mostly empty page.

Then another.

And still another.

There are squiggles.

There are doodles.

But the words won't come.

It's hard sometimes
not to give up

and walk away.

It's easier
(and usually more fun)
just to savor and enjoy
all the deliciously splendid tales
other writers have told.

But other people's stories
aren't exactly yours.

So it's still here:

an empty page,
waiting,
still calling

to you.

You make up your mind
to try again.

Maybe a cookie will help.

You eat it at the window, nibbling like a tiny bird

to make it last.

And that's when you notice . . .

. . . the chickadee.

He's been there all along.

But now you pay attention.
You watch him
visit the winter feeder,
plucking one
single,
tiny black seed
at a time.

You see how he swoops away
from the crowd
to eat in safety and peace
on a nearby branch.
This is how he makes a meal.
Just one seed.
And then another.

It's hard work.

It takes so much
energy,
concentration,
commitment.

But he's determined.
He doesn't give up.
He comes back
again and again.

Just one seed.
And then another.

And then
you look over
at the empty page.

Your page.

You go back,
pick up your pencil,

and begin.

Just one word.
And then another.

Now it's *your* turn!

This book ends with the boy about to write a story called
The Chickadee. Can you tell or write that story?
Here are some ideas to get you started, but it's up to you. After all,
it's your story. Remember, if you get stuck, maybe a cookie will help.

THE BEGINNING

Ideas for showing what the chickadee wants to do.

One cold day, a hungry chickadee flew to the feeder, but . . .

The chickadee loved sunflower seeds. But whenever . . .

"May I have turn?" asked the chickadee. The bigger birds . . .

THE MIDDLE

Ideas for showing how the chickadee struggles.

The feeder was so crowded, the chickadee . . .

The chickadee tried and tried, but . . .

"Move out of my way," the blue jay said . . .

THE END

Ideas for showing how the chickadee finds a way.

Suddenly, the chickadee had an idea . . .

Just when he was about to give up, the chickadee . . .

Suddenly, a friendly robin swooped down and said . . .

Read more about black-capped chickadees at the National Audubon Society
www.audubon.org/field-guide/bird/black-capped-chickadee

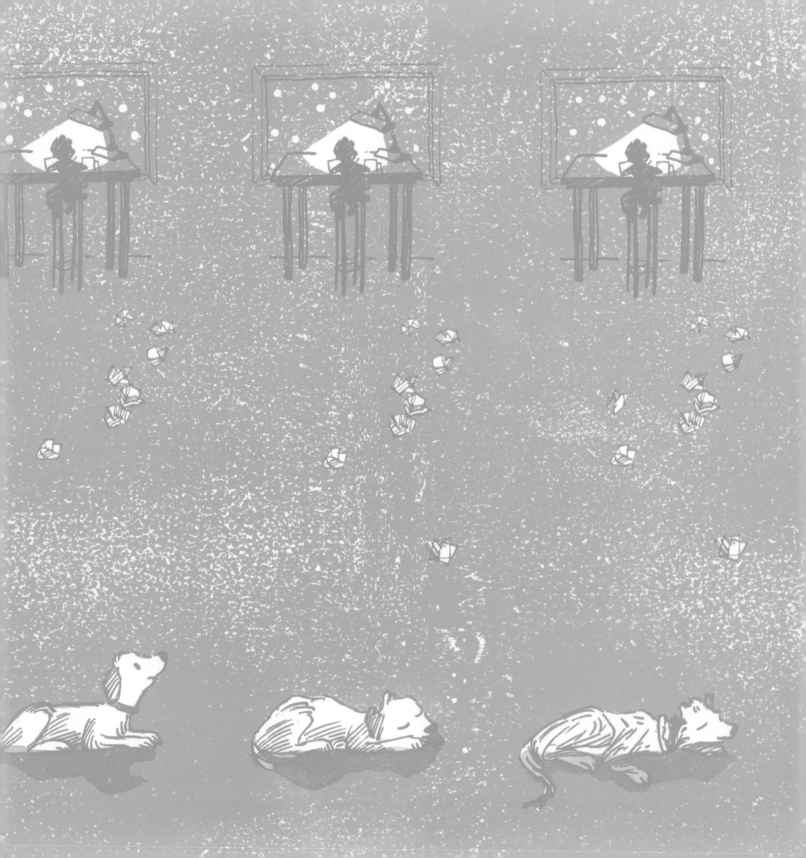